THE
DEVELOPING PEOPLE
POCKETBOOK

By Ian Fleming

Drawings by Phil Hailstone

"Very user-friendly, informative and thought provoking. A must for managers involved in, or with, training."
Mary Douglas, Production Director, Seven Seas

"Brimming with common sense for a painless approach to developing others."
Jacqueline Smith, Global Support Chain Capability Manager, Wyeth

Published by:
Management Pocketbooks Ltd
Laurel House, Station Approach, Alresford, Hants SO24 9JH, U.K.
Tel: +44 (0)1962 735573   Fax: +44 (0)1962 733637
E-mail: sales@pocketbook.co.uk
Website: www.pocketbook.co.uk

1st edition published as The Manager's Training Pocketbook

This 2nd edition published 2001 as The Developing People Pocketbook.
Reprinted 2003, 2004, 2006, 2007, 2009.

© Ian Fleming 1994, 2001

ISBN 978 1 870471 96 1

Design, typesetting and graphics by **efex ltd**   Printed in U.K.

CONTENTS

Author's note

This is the second edition of the book, and with it a change of title from 'The Manager's Training Pocketbook' to 'The Developing People Pocketbook'.

Training can often have a narrow focus, with the teaching of specific subjects or skills. Development is broader and embraces all learning experiences, both formal and informal. It's not simply about sending people on courses.

Most development opportunities take place at work and not on courses. Managers can make it happen – this book will show you how.

Ian Fleming

Ian Fleming

1 INTRODUCTION

INTRODUCTION

WHO THIS BOOK IS FOR

This book is written for those responsible for ensuring that staff in organisations are trained.

Traditionally, responsibility has been with those in formal positions, such as management development specialists or training managers. However, most learning opportunities happen on a daily basis in the workplace.

So if you're a manager, supervisor, departmental/section head or team leader then this book is for you. You may have training as part of your job responsibilities or perhaps you occasionally put together training sessions for your own team.

It aims to give you the basic skills to spot where your people need help and to put together suitable training. Should all you get out of it be knowing what to look for, then it will have served its purpose!

TRAINING OR DEVELOPMENT?

In a changing world - where insecurity is common and the future uncertain - responsibility for developing skills and managing careers rests with the individual.

The onus has shifted towards **self development**.

It is more relevant to talk about **learning and development** (results and outputs) than simply training and education (which are about inputs). It's been said that you train animals to jump over fences, but develop people!

Training using formal courses can be one way of developing staff, but don't rely on it being the only one.

WHY BOTHER TO DEVELOP?

Reasons against:

There are plenty of people on the job market. *(True, but how many have the skills and experience you need?)*

Not every organisation trains its staff. *(Again true, but increasingly people are coming to expect training as part of their job.)*

Many organisations see training as an investment with a long term payoff – and they are not prepared to wait. So they buy in the skills needed. *(With skills shortages this strategy is increasingly unrealistic.)*

Training people doesn't guarantee that they will stay; often they take their new skills and knowledge elsewhere. *(Sure this happens. However people who join your organisation have often received training and had experiences elsewhere.)*

When times are difficult many organisations put their investment of time, energies and money elsewhere, not in training.

INTRODUCTION

REASONS FOR DEVELOPING

RESPONDING TO CHANGE

You need to develop people to survive in and respond to a changing world.

Consider:

- The pace and nature of change in our lives and organisations
- The demands and expectations of customers that often lead to:
    - greater customer focus
    - radical ways of operating
    - cost savings
    - greater flexibility of people in the workplace
    - changing shapes of organisations, fewer levels, broader jobs, reduced 'resources'
    - uncertainty about the future/less job security

All these have implications for people's jobs and how they do them.

Successful organisations will always be those that help their people respond to and meet the challenges surrounding change.

REASONS FOR DEVELOPING

RESPONDING TO BUSINESS NEEDS

So how do you justify a spend on development especially when there are other priorities and pressures to consider?

To survive, organisations need to:

- Be customer focused
- Provide quality products or services
- Learn to trust and empower their staff

The key to delivering this is having staff who:

- Know what's expected of them and why
- Have the skills, confidence and support from their managers

REASONS FOR DEVELOPING

IGNORANCE IS EXPENSIVE

The lack of trained staff costs organisations dearly through:

- Mistakes and wasted materials/efforts
- Demotivated staff
- High staff turnover

And, more importantly ...

- Unhappy customers who often go elsewhere
- A poor reputation in the market place

WHOSE JOB IS IT?

Training and development are the responsibility of everyone in an organisation, not just those in formal training positions.

Starting at the top with the **chief executive/managing director** who:

- Provides the vision of where the organisation needs to be
- Sets an example by his/her leadership, and thereby ...
- Creates within the organisation the desire to achieve

Continuing with the **managers/supervisors** who are:

- Closest to the staff (often in day to day contact)
- In a position to spot a need and influence performance

Finally, it is also the responsibility of the **individuals** to:

- Take control of their own learning and manage their careers

DEVELOPMENT IN CONTEXT

Bear in mind the following points:

- Training and development is going on all the time
- The solving of everyday problems and situations is as much a part of the learning process as any training course
- Training is not an end in itself; on its own it produces no business results. It needs to focus on and be responsive to organisational strategies, and make a contribution towards their achievement
- Development is an investment but is also a cost
- Its contribution to the business must be thought through

THE COSTS

Whilst ignoring development has its price, any formal training has a cost. Remember – **training isn't cheap**. Before embarking on any training initiative, consider the costs of:

- **Your time**
  - to put it together and be involved
- **Participants**
  - the time they will spend attending
  - travel and, possibly, accommodation
  - arranging cover for their jobs whilst they are away
  - loss of business (opportunity costs)

- **Providing a venue**
  - hire of room and equipment (videos, computers, projectors)
  - food and refreshments
- **External help**
  - for example, consultants' fees and expenses
- **Getting it wrong**

What's more, management training often has a higher unit cost than any other type of training.

RECOGNISING
DEVELOPMENT NEEDS

THE NEED FOR ACCURACY

Accurately identifying needs is the first and most important step in putting together any training and development initiative.

Carried out properly, it will increase the chances of:

- Putting together appropriate help where necessary
- Measuring the impact of any help on performance and business objectives

Time, effort and money are very often wasted if the needs have been poorly diagnosed. So ask yourself:

- What do people **need** in order to do their jobs in a different way and/or with more confidence?

Note: Not all 'needs' can be met by training. Some may require a change in the way that the business is run or a fresh look at existing policies and practices.

PLACES TO LOOK

Training and development needs can arise in many ways:

- Through the setting of objectives
- From appraisals and reviews of performance
- As a result of mistakes being made
- From poor performance, ie: failure to reach standard
- Observing people in action
- Individuals asking for help
- Customer complaints
- The time taken to do a job
- Changes in:
  - legislation
  - work methods, systems, procedures
  - job content and responsibilities

WILL IT ADD VALUE?

- Resources (people's time and your money) are too valuable to waste, so **only train if you have to**.

- Training should be measured against the benefits to the organisation, ie: if we develop people's skills how will it add value to the business?

- Remember to consider non-training alternatives (where appropriate), eg: making changes to the systems or re-designing the jobs that people do.

NEEDS IDENTIFICATION

In simple terms, needs can be identified on the following levels:

RECOGNISING DEVELOPMENT NEEDS

QUESTIONNAIRE

Consider the following as a guide to identifying needs, adding your own examples where necessary.

Ask yourself what **needs** you have in your organisation (or department) under the following headings:

CUSTOMERS

Rate the importance of each item on a scale ranging from 1 (low) to 10 (high)

1	2	3	4	5	6	7	8	9	10

- Improve the quality of your products
- Introduce new products/services
- Attract new customers
- Improve customer service
- Retain existing customers
- ....
- ....
- ....
- ....

RECOGNISING DEVELOPMENT NEEDS

QUESTIONNAIRE

FINANCIAL

- Improve overall profitability
- Reduce costs
- Improve cash flow
- Make better use of financial data
- Improve financial/business planning
- Budget for future activities
- ....
- ....
- ....

Rate the importance of each item on a scale ranging from 1 (low) to 10 (high)

1	2	3	4	5	6	7	8	9	10
1	2	3	4	5	6	7	8	9	10
1	2	3	4	5	6	7	8	9	10
1	2	3	4	5	6	7	8	9	10
1	2	3	4	5	6	7	8	9	10
1	2	3	4	5	6	7	8	9	10
1	2	3	4	5	6	7	8	9	10
1	2	3	4	5	6	7	8	9	10
1	2	3	4	5	6	7	8	9	10

RECOGNISING DEVELOPMENT NEEDS

QUESTIONNAIRE

PEOPLE

Rate the importance of each item on a scale ranging from 1 (low) to 10 (high)

- Reduce turnover
- Improve morale
- Increase the skills and confidence of staff
- Redesign jobs
- Encourage job flexibility
- Improve communications at all levels
- Coping with existing and planned changes
- Identifying and developing talent
- ....
- ....
- ....

1	2	3	4	5	6	7	8	9	10
1	2	3	4	5	6	7	8	9	10
1	2	3	4	5	6	7	8	9	10
1	2	3	4	5	6	7	8	9	10
1	2	3	4	5	6	7	8	9	10
1	2	3	4	5	6	7	8	9	10
1	2	3	4	5	6	7	8	9	10
1	2	3	4	5	6	7	8	9	10
1	2	3	4	5	6	7	8	9	10
1	2	3	4	5	6	7	8	9	10
1	2	3	4	5	6	7	8	9	10

QUESTIONNAIRE

LEGISLATION

Rate the importance of each item on a scale ranging from 1 (low) to 10 (high)

- Ensure that current legislation is complied with
- Plan for the introduction of new legislation
- ....
- ....
- ....

1	2	3	4	5	6	7	8	9	10
1	2	3	4	5	6	7	8	9	10
1	2	3	4	5	6	7	8	9	10
1	2	3	4	5	6	7	8	9	10
1	2	3	4	5	6	7	8	9	10

I.T.

- Introduce new systems
- Raise the levels of I.T. skills/awareness
- ....

1	2	3	4	5	6	7	8	9	10
1	2	3	4	5	6	7	8	9	10
1	2	3	4	5	6	7	8	9	10

RECOGNISING DEVELOPMENT NEEDS

QUESTIONNAIRE
ANALYSIS

Now note the 5 items that you have scored the highest.

1. ....

2. ....

3. ....

4. ....

5. ....

- Will acquiring knowledge and skills help meet these needs?
- If you answer 'Yes' to any, then you have a potential training need.
- If the answer is 'No', you may have to find ways of meeting the need other than training.

Adapted from Tad Leduchowicz in 'Improving Trainer Effectiveness', published by Gower.

IDENTIFYING INDIVIDUAL NEEDS

As well as identifying organisational/departmental needs, you need to be able to analyse the performance of your staff, eg:

- If your people are not performing to the standard expected of them, then why is this?
- In what areas do staff need to improve?
- Is training or some other action the answer to performance improvement?

The following pages contain a practical way of identifying the action that can be taken to improve individual performance.

ASSESSING PERFORMANCE

Potentially you have a lot of data with which to gauge a person's performance.

- Look at the job description to identify the areas of skills, knowledge and experience required to do the job satisfactorily.

- Consider any objectives that have been set for the individual.

- In which of the above areas is the person not performing adequately?

- Are any of these shortfalls caused by the fact that they lack skills, knowledge and/or experience?

If the answer is 'Yes', then action such as appropriate training, coaching or job rotation needs to be taken.

If it is 'No', then other action needs to be taken such as that outlined in the Performance Flowchart, which follows.

PERFORMANCE FLOWCHART

Are performance shortfalls caused by a lack of skills, knowledge and experience? — **YES** All or some → Look to fill the gap with training and coaching

NO

Are policies and procedures preventing desired performance? — **YES** → Re-examine policy/procedures to help not hinder

NO

Is some obstacle (lack of resources/equipment, time) preventing desired performance? — **YES** → Provide resources / Lower standards / Remove obstacles

NO

Are colleagues, bosses, management style, blocking desired performance? — **YES** → Deal with individuals / Train and educate to encourage a different style

NO

Is my advice ignored/disregarded? — **YES** → Find out why / Ask for feedback / Try a different approach

NO

Repeat analysis – examine performance data, etc

With thanks to John Townsend

23

AVOID GENERALISATION

As a result of the previous exercises, you may have identified say, 'financial awareness', 'managing staff' and 'improving communications skills' as areas for improvement. These descriptions are too broad to be helpful.

Consider what skills might be involved in each.

- Financial awareness could include:
  - the ability to put together a budget for your department
  - understanding the breakdown of costs and their application to your business
  - being able to read, understand and use financial data/information
- Managing staff might involve:
  - recognising the talents and abilities of your staff
  - setting objectives for both groups and individuals
  - maintaining team spirit while under pressure

RECOGNISING DEVELOPMENT NEEDS

AVOID GENERALISATION

Communication skills could call for the ability to:

- Present information, both formally and informally, to groups
- 'Sell' decisions made by others to your staff
- Accurately listen to the views of others and, where appropriate, feed them back to selected individuals

All three are very broad areas, open to a variety of interpretations and, without clarification, are of little practical use.

It pays, therefore, to be as precise as possible when identifying needs.

RECOGNISING DEVELOPMENT NEEDS

AVOID GENERALISATION

When you are looking for training to meet any needs, it helps to be as **specific** as possible.

In so doing, you will eventually save time and money as needs can often be met in ways other than sending people on courses. (See pages 45-54 for examples.)

Any Learning and Development/Talent Management Department will ask you to be more precise. So probe behind any general statements for a more accurate description. Then you should be in a position to take some meaningful action.

Tip: Look at job descriptions for details of knowledge and skills that individuals need. Alternatively, initiatives (in the UK) such as Management Charter and (S)NVQ can be used as the basis for identifying abilities and spotting needs.

LEARNING GAP

Accurate identification of **needs** will reveal a **learning gap** between present knowledge and skills, and the desired level.

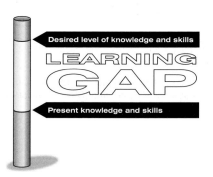

Identify the gap with those involved. This will help motivation and ownership.

- Why do they think that it has occurred?
- How do they think that the gap can be closed?
- What support do they want and from whom?

27

NOTES

NEEDS INTO OBJECTIVES

REASONS FOR OBJECTIVES

Having identified a need, try turning it into a learning objective. In other words, what **noticeable behaviour** will you see when the learning has taken place?

Why? As a basis for:

- Ensuring that the training reflects the needs of your organisation
- Measuring the outcome of any learning (otherwise how will you know that you have achieved the desired result?)
- Motivating the learner to **know** what they have to achieve
- Demonstrating the payoff to organisation and individual
- Preparing a cost benefit analysis
- Starting the design of any training

WRITING LEARNING OBJECTIVES

Objectives are needed to show what, at the end of the learning, individuals will:

- Know, eg: how to organise a project
- Be able to do (that requires the acquisition or development of **skills**), eg: be able to persuade, assemble, draw, etc

To each of these needs to be added some form of **measurement** of the effective behaviour. There may also be times when you have to describe the conditions under which people are expected to operate.

Note: Beware of objectives where you want to improve or change attitudes. Attitudes often show themselves in people's behaviour and it is this that you need to concentrate on changing or adapting.

WRITING LEARNING OBJECTIVES

While you may feel somewhat apprehensive about doing this, it's no different from setting objectives at appraisal time.

Take the need that you have identified and ask:

- What has to be done?
- To what standard?
- By when?

Concentrate on what the **end result** of the actions will be and use verbs and/or action words such as:

- describe, identify, organise
- assemble, persuade, show

It is acceptable to have more than one verb or action word in an objective.

NEEDS INTO OBJECTIVES

EXAMPLE: TIME MANAGEMENT

1. Identify the need

You have identified a need for people to improve their use and management of time. You have noticed individuals:

- Working long hours
- Getting side-tracked by interruptions
- Taking on too many jobs
- Failing to meet deadlines

EXAMPLE: TIME MANAGEMENT

2. Establish the evidence

If you are looking for some training in this area, then ask yourself what you will accept as evidence that it has been successful? What you come up with **is** the objective.

An example of evidence could be that individuals will:

Know
- The basic principles of managing their time
- How to organise both themselves and others
- How to select objectives/priorities on which to work

Be able to
- Prioritise their work
- Organise themselves to achieve priorities
- Record and analyse how their time is spent
- Deal effectively with interruptions

NEEDS INTO OBJECTIVES

EXAMPLE: TIME MANAGEMENT

3. Write the objectives

Objectives for training in this area might look as follows.

At the end of the course individuals will be able to:

- Establish the content of their jobs and will have identified three priority objectives to achieve over the next three months
- Devise plans for achieving these objectives with key dates identified in their diaries
- Operate a system for examining their use of time, and state ways in which they can take control over their daily activities

EXAMPLE: PROBLEM SOLVING/CREATIVITY

1. Identify the need

You need to help people improve their skills in dealing with problems and thinking afresh.

This has become evident through:

- Lack of new ideas coming forward within the organisation
- Groups spending a lot of time dealing with the symptoms of problems and failing to get to the root cause (drowning in problems)
- The organisation's need for new products/services in order to keep ahead of the market

EXAMPLE: PROBLEM SOLVING/CREATIVITY

2. Establish the evidence

Evidence of success might be that individuals will:

Know
- How to apply a structured approach to solving problems
- How to distinguish between the symptoms of a problem and its cause
- A range of creativity techniques to help them generate ideas

Be able to
- Identify the causes of problems using a structured approach
- Use a range of techniques to generate new ideas for tackling situations
- Sell their ideas to others effectively

NEEDS INTO OBJECTIVES

EXAMPLE: PROBLEM SOLVING/CREATIVITY

3. Write the objectives

Possible objectives for a course would be as follows.

At the end of the course individuals will:

- Be able to recognise the benefits that being creative can bring (to both the organisation and the jobs they do)
- Have identified three areas where fresh thinking can be applied to their jobs
- Be able to apply a structured approach to a current business problem/opportunity and have generated a minimum of three new ways of tackling it
- Plan how they are going to sell their ideas to others upon their return to work

OBJECTIVES NOT AIMS

Don't worry if you're not a training specialist – in fact it sometimes helps if you're not! What's more, don't shy away from writing objectives. Remember to keep them simple and ask yourself:

- What's the need? How has it arisen?
- How will I know that the training has been successful?
- What do I want people to do at the end?

When looking at any (commercial) training proposal, make sure that the objectives are expressed in terms of behavioural outcomes. If not, then ask the provider to explain how you will know that their training has been successful.

Very often what are stated as objectives are really aims.
Aims are directions, objectives are destinations.

NEEDS INTO OBJECTIVES

CHECKLIST

- Take time to identify what people actually **need** to do their jobs better

- Make sure that you can express it in everyday language

- Ask yourself what you want people to be able to do as a result of the training

- Establish evidence of success

- Try writing some draft objectives

  - check them against the need and evidence of success you have identified

  - should they not quite fit, then try again

FINDING LEARNING OPPORTUNITIES

FINDING LEARNING OPPORTUNITIES

LEARNING IS ALL AROUND US

- Both life and work offer endless opportunities to learn. But organisations frequently restrict themselves to course or classroom learning activities (despite the fact that they often don't work)

- Look for opportunities both on and off the job (see next page)

- What you choose will depend on a variety of factors:
  - the precise nature of the need
  - timescale ... how urgent it is
  - availability of people to give and receive any planned help
  - costs involved, facilities required
  - preferred style of the learner (see pages 85-88 on learning style)

FINDING LEARNING OPPORTUNITIES

WITHIN WORK

Learning opportunities at work include:

Within the job

- Attending meetings
- Projects
- Making a presentation
- Acting as a spokesperson
- Writing a report
- Visiting a supplier
- Showing people around

Extending the job

- Standing in for somebody
- Shadowing/work experience
- Job sharing
- Some form of exchange
- Secondment
- Job rotation

FINDING LEARNING OPPORTUNITIES

WITHIN WORK

Working with others
- Passing on skills/experience to others
- Being part of a project team, task force, quality circle
- Introducing a change
- Putting together a training programme
- Being involved in negotiations

Extra responsibility
- Taking on additional tasks
- Setting something up
- Closing something down
- Being promoted

As well as ...
- Watching somebody in action (an expert or skilled performer)
- Spending time with an expert
- Being thrown in at the deep end
- Crises
- Successes and disasters

TECHNIQUES

The following pages set out some of the methods that can be used to develop your people.

1. Coaching

Improving performance at work by turning the things that people do into learning situations in a planned way under guidance.

Pros

Suitable for both individuals and teams
Focus is on events that actually occur
Tailored to suit needs of individuals
Encourages people to use the skills in real life situations

Cons

Can take time to bring about improvements
People sometimes forget that coaching and instructing are different
Will not work if the relationship between both parties lacks trust

TECHNIQUES

2. Action learning

Where groups of individuals come together to work on existing organisational problems.

Pros

Involves those who own problems and are best qualified to solve them
Best opportunity to develop individuals is in their own organisation
Is action based and immediate, not concerned with making future recommendations

Cons

It needs a certain amount of structure to work well
Relies on people being open and prepared to share their situations with others
Possibly suffers from an image problem – it is not as widely used as it could be

TECHNIQUES

3. Role rehearsals (role plays)

A technique used to rehearse the skills needed in certain situations.

Pros

Enables people to play out solutions and possible
approaches. If you make 'mistakes' it doesn't matter –
just avoid them when going 'live'. Can be used for a
variety of situations, eg: practising a skill,
demonstrating a situation or trying out
intended actions.

Cons

Individuals may need to be coached
through situations to get the most out of
them. Some people aren't natural actors
and find the situations difficult. Not
everyone's preferred style of learning.

TECHNIQUES

4. Internal courses

Where individuals from the same organisation come together to develop their skills and abilities.

Pros

Possible to train a large number of people at one time
Content can be geared to the organisation
Can help shape opinions and work towards changing attitudes
Aids promotion of a common message

Cons

People often see it as a chance to moan about the organisation
No exposure to 'fresh thinking' from fellow participants outside organisation
Without help and support from managers, there's no guarantee that knowledge and skills will be applied

TECHNIQUES

5. External courses

Attended by people from a variety of organisations.

Pros

Exposure to fresh thinking
Chance to meet new people and share ideas
Can make people appreciate what a good organisation they work for!

Cons

Can be expensive
Content may be too general to be relevant
No guarantee that ideas gained can be applied without support from
within the organisation

TECHNIQUES

6. Delegating tasks

Whereby a manager gives up part of his/her job to another person.

Pros

Shows trust and confidence in the individual
Frees the manager to do more valuable work
Useful way of developing – with guidance – the skills of staff

Cons

Is hard work and requires confidence and faith in others
Involves committing time in the short term for a longer term payoff
With heavy workloads, people may be reluctant to take on delegated work

TECHNIQUES

7. DVD

On a particular topic relevant to the organisation or a job.

Pros

Can be entertaining and informative. Multi-use for a large number of people.
Can be shown at any time of the day/night as well as in work/non-work locations.

Cons

Expensive to produce or
buy. Not everybody finds
them of interest. No
guarantee that individuals
will be able to identify with
the situation or apply the
messages.

51

TECHNIQUES

8. Project

A study into any aspect of what you do or how you do things in your business.

Pros

Can be conducted by teams or individuals
Usually has a defined time limit and provides variety from daily tasks
Allows for real improvements to take place in the way you run your business

Cons

Can fail through lack of guidelines, terms of reference and clear deadlines
'Projects' are seen as the answer to every business situation
People may be too busy to give sufficient time to the project

TECHNIQUES

9. Open or flexible learning

A generic term used to refer to a wide range of approaches, where the learner has a choice over what and how they learn, as well as the pace and the time.

It is a fast developing area that embraces a range of learning approaches, including:

- Using technology, eg: e-learning, interactive video and CD-Rom
- Desk-based audio and video learning
- Workbooks

Off-the-shelf programmes are available from an increasing number of suppliers. Alternatively, it is possible to have materials produced to suit your own needs.

Open or flexible learning is not tutor-free. Help is needed to explain and encourage, support and guide the learner. This calls for different skills from that of the *up-front* classroom presenter.

TECHNIQUES

10. E-learning

Potentially e-learning has a lot of advantages, including being able to train vast numbers of people (where regulatory compliance is needed), track individual progress and achieve cost-savings.

However, in reality, e-learning initiatives work best when:

- They are tied in with learning goals that are relevant to the business and can be monitored/measured

- The technology itself does not prove a barrier to learning by either being out-of-date or prone to breakdown

- It's part of a range of learning methods that are used and one that is actually interactive and engages the learner

- People get the chance to share their learning with others in similar situations

- Methods are in place for evaluating the learning, and not simply the number of users on the system

TRANSFER OF LEARNING

A note of caution!

- Whatever the method you use, do not assume that people will **automatically** be able to use their new-found knowledge and skills in their own situation. It is not always that easy. So ...

- When selecting methods think also about how you plan to ensure that people transfer any learning gained to the work situation

- Do this by ensuring that:
  - the training situations and the job are similar
  - there's a link between the training and the job that they are/will be doing
  - there's a payoff for using the knowledge and skills gained in the workplace, in other words improved ways of doing things
  - people are encouraged to try out the skills learnt **sooner rather than later**

INCREASING TRANSFER OF LEARNING

Assuming that the methods chosen meet the individual's needs, the potential for transferring learning can be increased in each of the areas:

Coaching
Watch people in action and give further ideas and encouragement

Action learning
Give individuals the chance to try out new ideas and approaches

Role play
Make the situations as real as possible

Courses (internal and external)
Be clear in advance about content; make sure that pre and post course briefings take place, and encourage people to use what they have learnt

Delegation
Invest time when people are learning new tasks

Watching a DVD
Carefully select the DVD; link any message in it to the needs of organisation/individual

Project
Select a project that will make a difference to the way you do business and set clear guidelines and timescales

Open and e-learning
Look for opportunities where people can use their knowledge and skills with support from yourself

PREPARING
FOR LEARNING

PREPARING FOR LEARNING

BRIEFING THE LEARNER

WHAT <u>NOT</u> TO DO

1. You pass on details of a training event without:
   - understanding what it is about
   - checking the relevance to both the individual and their job
   - talking to the individual

2. The individual attends:
   - not knowing why they are there
   - anti or indifferent to the learning (a trainer's nightmare)
   - seeing no relevance in the topics or their applications
   - disrupting the event with negative comments, eg: 'You should tell all this to my boss, not me'
   - feeling slightly inferior to others who clearly are there for a purpose

3. The result is a:
   - negative experience for all concerned
   - waste of time and money
   - missed opportunity for real learning to take place

BRIEFING THE LEARNER

WHAT TO DO

As a manager you need to be involved in briefing your people. After all:

- You may have helped identify the need and come up with a solution

- As part of your role as a coach you need to ensure that your staff have the opportunity to **use** any knowledge and skills gained when they return to work

- Without the chance to practise and apply (under your guidance) any new-found learning it will all have been a wasted effort

- Who knows – you too may learn something!

So, the message is **get involved!** Don't rely on the training department to do it for you; you could have to wait a long time!

BRIEFING THE LEARNER

WHAT TO TELL THEM

If you are sending people away on any training, internal or external, they need to know:

- What has been arranged for them, in what areas and in what form
- The reasons why, eg: how it might link with possible changes taking place, appraisal discussions, requests for help, career development, etc
- How it is designed to help them, what the links are between the learning and the practical application
- What it will involve (content, style of learning, action plans)
- Where the learning will take place (venue, timing, dates, expenses and, if relevant, travel arrangements and accommodation)
- Any reporting back that is to take place
- What help they will get, on return, to apply the learning

Note: If you are unable to answer any of these questions then go back and ask the provider of the training. Remember, training is not cheap.

BRIEFING THE LEARNER

BEFORE A COURSE

Some organisations ask you to complete nomination forms prior to attending any training event.

The aim is to involve you as a manager by ensuring that you have briefed your staff about what to expect.

I have seen the following training nomination form used to good effect for those attending formal training courses.

If your training department doesn't have a similar form, why not suggest that they use this one?

PREPARING FOR LEARNING

TRAINING NOMINATION FORM

Instructions
Form to be completed by the nominated manager.
Discussed with the member of staff and their responses noted.
Returned to the training department <u>by the date specified</u>.

Name   Department

Position   Date(s)

Course title

1. Reasons for nominating the above for the course are to: Yes/No
   a) Improve the skills needed for their present job   Yes/No
   b) Provide a broader understanding and knowledge of the subject area Yes/No
   c) Personal development

Any other reasons

TRAINING NOMINATION FORM

2. Has the member of staff been informed of:
   a) The course title and objectives — Yes/No
   b) Why they have been selected to attend — Yes/No

3. Is the member of staff:
   a) Enthusiastic about attending — Yes/No
   b) Indifferent about attending ** — Yes/No
   c) Reluctant to attend — Yes/No
   d) Other (please comment)

   ** If the answer to b) or c) is 'Yes', could you expand on the reasons

4. Has the individual had any previous instruction or training in the subject
   matter covered by the course? — Yes/No
   If the answer is 'Yes', then please give an indication of the level and extent so
   that the training can be matched to experience

63

TRAINING NOMINATION FORM

5. What do you expect the learning to do for your member of staff and why?

6. How do you plan to ensure that these expectations are met?

7. What plans have you agreed with the member of staff to enable them to use the skills and/or knowledge they have learnt back in the workplace?

Please return completed form to (nominated person) by (date).

BRIEFING THE TRAINER

As a manager, the chances are that you are paying for the costs of the training out of your budget. Your interests, therefore, are to make sure that you get what you want. So **talk** to the person delivering the training.

Any trainer worth their salt will want to know:

- The big picture, ie: what's happening in the organisation, any current or potential issues that might be raised in the training (it may help them to make links between the training and the bigger picture)
- Who is attending
    - what jobs they do and where
    - any relevant information about their background, skills and previous experiences; whether or not they all know one another
    - why they have been nominated to attend and what they want out of it, plus any concerns that may have been expressed

RUNNING A COURSE

If you have organised a course for your staff, then it's worth being around at the start to:

- Ensure that the rooms are set up as requested, that handouts and notes are available

- Welcome people and show them where things are

- Make sure that any planned refreshments have arrived

- Make contact with the speaker

- Formally introduce the speaker, explain any in-house routines, including the taking of messages, mobile phones, etc

RUNNING A COURSE

It will pay you to check during the day to see:

- How the speaker is performing
- If he/she is doing what was agreed
- How people are reacting to the speaker and to each other
- What the mood is (try joining them for lunch, although don't expect much useful information on the learning to emerge at this stage)

Then make sure that you are there at the end to:

- Wrap it up
- Gain the views of the participants (again, don't expect too much as it may be too soon and people often do their thinking on the journey home)
- Talk things through with the tutors
- Be aware of any contentious views that have emerged from or during the day

RECAP

To get a return from your investment, do what you can to make people aware of:

- What has been arranged for them and why
- How it will help them in their jobs
- What help they will be given to apply the learning

Remember that if you're buying in training, then you are the customer and are in the driving seat. So **you** ask the questions.

Finally, don't rely on luck. Both manager and trainers (in organisations) have a role to play in preparing people for learning.

Who to use

INTERNAL

If you need to put together any training, don't ignore the people you have within your own organisation.

Pros
- They will know the organisation, its culture and often the people
- Cost – they are already on the payroll
- Saves time – needs can often be met sooner rather than later
- By sharing their knowledge and expertise they also develop their own skills

Cons
- Can be too familiar with people
- Too busy – may have insufficient time to prepare
- May not be trained as 'teachers' – could be technically sound but poor at putting it across
- Not necessarily good role models – 'Do as I say not as I do'

INTERNAL
SEE THEM IN ACTION

Don't give up on the idea of using your own people –
including yourself. After all:

- People can be trained to 'teach'. The Management
  Pocketbook Series has many excellent titles to help
  – see the title listing at the back of the book

- If you do use internal resources, then:
    - try to see them in action (how
      good are they at 'helping'?)
    - make sure that they know what
      your people **need** to know and
      to be able to do
    - jointly explore the best ways
      of making this happen

USING OUTSIDERS

10 QUESTIONS TO ASK

Bringing people in from outside can be both expensive and risky. It's an area where it is easy to make mistakes, waste an awful lot of money and get it badly wrong.

However, if you get it right then there are many benefits to be gained on both sides. As with identifying needs, it pays to devote time to selecting the right providers. Read behind the glossy brochures and make sure you ask the following questions:

1. What are they offering (standard courses, tailor-made, computer assisted learning, etc)? How far does it meet your needs?

2. What is their knowledge and understanding of your business and the market in which you operate? (This is not a pre-requisite but often a useful indicator to see how much they have bothered to find out about your organisation.)

USING OUTSIDERS

10 QUESTIONS TO ASK

3. Concerning any proposal that they put forward:
   - does it make sense?
   - what does it cover, and how far does it reflect any brief that you have given them?

4. Who will be involved in delivering any training?
   - what are their credentials and experience?
   - what back up is there, should there be a problem?

5. If you are not talking to the training deliverer, when will you meet him or her?

USING OUTSIDERS

10 QUESTIONS TO USE

6. Of the organisation (and indeed the individual)
   - what are they known for?
   - what have they researched, written and had published?

7. Learning methods
   - how do they teach? (suitable for all styles?)
   - what materials do they use and how relevant are they? (some of the motivation theories are pretty old and the research data rather suspect)

8. Who else have they done similar work for?
   - what **exactly** did they do, when, where?
   - who can you contact in that organisation so that you can hear **their** version of how it went?

USING OUTSIDERS

10 QUESTIONS TO ASK

9.   What will it cost?
  - for any fees quoted, what **exactly** is included?
  - hidden costs could include
    * development work
    * putting together the proposal
    * visits and attending meetings
    * travel (at what rate – yours or theirs?)
    * accommodation (what will you pay for?)
    * 'expenses': what does this include/not include?
    * has the meter already started?
  - don't forget to add on any tax
  - does it sound good value for money?
  - how far will it stack up against any cost/benefit analysis?

USING OUTSIDERS

10 QUESTIONS TO ASK

10. What are they going to do to find out about your organisation **at their expense?**

Finally, a question for you. What's your 'gut reaction' about them and their organisation? Are they credible? Could you and your people work with them – how will they be accepted?

BEWARE OF EXPERTS

There are plenty of so-called 'experts' offering help. Be on your guard against:

- The glossy brochure with stage-managed photos
  - people in smart clothes
  - meaningless graphs on the flip charts
  - everybody paying attention to the charismatic tutor (not even **I** can hold attention like their presenters claim to!)

- The impressive client list
  - what **exactly** did they do, and for what parts of this (impressive) organisation
  - the promises and claims to do everything
  - the training flavour of the month
  - the salesperson who sells the concept or idea, that's delivered by someone else you have never met

WHERE TO FIND HELP

- They may well come to you via:
  - mailshots
  - speculative calls by phone or in person
  - contacts
  - recommendations
  - personal experience (you have seen them in action)

- You can get names from:
  - professional organisations, ie: Institute of Management Consultants and The Chartered Institute of Personnel and Development
  - your own contacts in other organisations
  - articles (or books) that they have written, publicising their success and skills
  - training directories in libraries, visits to trade fairs and exhibitions
  - the Internet

WHAT TO LOOK FOR IN A TRAINER

As a guide, look for individuals who can demonstrate:

1. Competence in and knowledge of the subject
2. The ability to put it across in a variety of situations
3. Concern/empathy for students' learning problems

The professional trainer will demonstrate a high level of skill in each of these areas, in particular finding time to:

- Empathise
- Adapt his or her material to groups or individuals
- Coach and counsel, even if it involves working through breaks and after sessions

MAINTAINING A FRESH APPROACH

If you have been using the same people every year to provide training for you, then clearly they have got to know your organisation and its needs. The danger, though, is that they might become complacent, stale and take you for granted.

So try putting your training out to tender every couple of years. Invite a range of people to suggest ways in which they would tackle your needs. This allows you to:

- Test the market and get fresh ideas
- Ask some of the questions suggested on pages 72-76
- Ensure that you are getting what your organisation needs
- Involve other managers in the selection process (if relevant)
- Keep your existing providers on their toes!

INCREASING YOUR CHANCES

INFLUENCING THE CONTENT

You can increase your chances of getting results from your training if you can get the trainer to deliver what your people need, as opposed to what he/she **likes** to deliver.

If training needs and objectives are based around the trainer's choices, sessions could well be:

- Formal and taught
- Well planned, yet follow a timetable
- Led from the front, with the needs of the learner secondary

By asking individuals what they want, and accommodating their requests, the **learner** becomes the centre of attention and, as a result, can become:

- More actively involved
- In control of what they learn, and
- Motivated to develop themselves

LEARNER CENTRED TRAINING

Learner centred training calls for:

- A different relationship between the 'trainer' (whether line manager or professional trainer) and trainee, eg: 'How can I help you?' as opposed to 'Listen to this ...'
- Less emphasis on the trainer's 'instructional' skills; more focus on a supportive, guiding, coaching, facilitating role

If you place more emphasis on self-development, the chances are that you could be sending fewer of your people on training courses and encouraging more 'open learning initiatives' and on-the-job opportunities.

DON'T MAKE ASSUMPTIONS

When arranging training for others, it is easy to make the mistake of assuming that what works for you will work for them.

So bear in mind that there may be differences in:

- Age
- Experience
- Position/status
- Skills, knowledge and experience
- Conditions under which you learnt and those at present
- Preferred learning styles (we all learn in different ways)

TRAINING FAILURES

WHAT WENT WRONG?

The following four case studies describe people who gained little from the training organised for them.

Person A:
A lively, outgoing individual, always keen to try new experiences. She was sent on a course that involved listening to lectures, reading the accompanying notes in a manual and watching videos.

Person B:
A quieter, more cautious, individual, with a preference for sitting back and watching others, preferring to think before acting. As part of his development he was sent on an outdoor leadership event. The course involved being selected at short notice to lead a team. Feedback on his performance was then given by both instructors and fellow team members.

TRAINING FAILURES

WHAT WENT WRONG?

Person C:
Could be described as a perfectionist, with a tendency to think things through in a logical step-by-step way, whilst questioning and probing the basic assumptions behind something.
As part of improving her relationships with others, she was asked to attend a sensitivity training programme. An integral part of this involved opening up to situations she was facing and talking through her feelings.

Person D:
Is practical and is always looking for new techniques or ideas to try out in the job.
He was sent on a business simulation course that involved making choices arising from situations that emerged throughout the three days. Individuals were not encouraged to make links between the content and their own jobs, but to gain an appreciation of how business works.

LEARNING STYLES

PREFERENCES REVEALED

Training often fails. The causes are varied, and many cannot be controlled. However, one potential problem area is if the method of learning to which individuals are exposed does not suit their preferred style. Honey and Mumford's work on learning styles identified:

- **Activists** (Person A) who:
  - learn best from short here-and-now tasks
  - try anything once and are enthusiastic about new activities
  - throw themselves into action-based courses, games and exercises, especially anything competitive

For Person A the style of training was too passive and did not allow enough participation.

- **Reflectors** (Person B) who:
  - learn best from standing back and observing what's happening
  - prefer to collect and analyse data before coming to conclusions
  - enjoy watching people in action

Person B was made to feel uncomfortable and did not learn from being thrust into a leadership position and then given feedback.

LEARNING STYLES

PREFERENCES REVEALED

- **Theorists** (Person C) who:
    - learn best when reviewing content in terms of a system, model or theory
    - tend to be detached and analytical
    - put great stock on rationality and logic

Person C learnt little when asked to share her innermost feelings with others.

- **Pragmatists** (Person D) who:
    - learn when there is an obvious link between the subject matter and a problem or opportunity on the job
    - search for new ideas and the chance to apply them to a relevant situation
    - like to get on with things, rather than have long open-ended discussions

Person D gained little from the training he described as 'too theoretical'.

IMPLICATIONS FOR LEARNING

If you are looking to organise training for others:

- Bear in mind your own preferences
  - don't let this influence how you organise learning for others – what works for you may not work for others

- Ask individuals for their own experiences of learning
  - this could give you a clue to their preferred style and, more importantly, influence the type of learning events you put together

Get hold of the Honey and Mumford *Learning Styles Questionnaire* and put your people through it before arranging any training. Ask your training department for a copy or see the reading list for details.

HELPING OLDER LEARNERS

If you are training older workers they may need something different. Should this be the case, then try to:

- Keep memorising to a minimum
- Use understanding as the basis for learning wherever possible
- With physical skills, concentrate on speed and accuracy, using simple tests
- Give practical experience before theory – if at all possible
- Use 'hands over' where precise physical movements are needed, ie: guide the hand
- Ensure a high success rate in the early stages of learning
- Arrange for an older learner to have an experienced worker as nominated 'friend'

DON'T FORGET

We have learnt to do many things in our lives, eg: in the home or by following some form of hobby or interest.

Hardly any of it takes place in a formal classroom situation.

INCREASING YOUR CHANCES

THE NEXT STEP

So, having taken action to increase your chances of success, you should now be in a position to run effective learning events.

However, this is **not** the end of the story.

You still have to work out how you are going to measure the impact on performance of what you have set up.

MEASURING THE IMPACT

WHAT HAPPENS IN PRACTICE

The chances are that you will have put a lot of time into planning and organising training. However, evaluating the impact that the training has had on performance is often given less consideration.

You could work for an organisation that:

- Uses 'tick in the box' (the categories of which are often so generalised as to be meaningless)
- Focuses more on the admin details than on what people have learnt
- Asks delegates to complete a form at the end of the training; the danger with this approach is that people are often in a hurry to leave and have simply 'had enough'

Or you could work for an organisation that simply does nothing at all!

You need to establish the evaluation criteria, plus the methods to be used, when you are setting objectives and designing any learning. In other words, at the <u>start</u> and not at the end as an afterthought.

ASSESSMENT OR EVALUATION?

There are two fundamental elements of training:

1. The quality of the training that takes place, ie: how much people enjoyed it, what exercises were used and the standard of the venue. The quality of these can be **assessed** by questionnaires and talking to participants.

2. The quality and value of what people have learnt as a result, ie: what learning has taken place, how people have changed and the personal benefits in terms of behaviour and performance. The value or worth of these can be **evaluated**.

For more information in this area read '*The Business of Training*' by Trevor Bentley, published by McGraw-Hill.

THE CASE FOR EVALUATION

Evaluating what has been learnt is extremely important. You may need it to demonstrate:

- The number of training days provided for your people
- The costs and benefits to the department/organisation
- The contribution that training has made in terms of:
  - the achievement of specific business or organisational goals
  - improvements in productivity and performance
  - impact on 'bottom line' where feasible

Don't forget to evaluate all forms of training, not just courses.

THE CASE FOR EVALUATION

You may also need objective evidence to:

- Compose a budget
- Justify expenditure and secure additional resources
- Identify what percentage of your salary costs are spent on training
- Make comparisons with other departments/organisations
- Publicise what you've done either internally or externally

As a manager you will want to know the return on your investment. You will always get comments about the venue, food or tutor. Far **more** value will be obtained from finding out about the quality of the learning that has resulted:

- What can they do now that they could not do before?
- What changes in performance has it produced that I can measure?
- Overall, was the effort worthwhile?

TECHNIQUES FOR EVALUATION

The value and worth of training can be measured both whilst learning is taking place and afterwards.

1. Within learning events

Aim: to find out what people are learning.

For example, use questionnaires:
- To identify what people know at the start of a learning event
- To check their understanding of learning points during an event
- To test what they have acquired at the end

A whole range of quizzes can be devised to recap any points made during the learning. These are often a lot of fun for participants, as well as serving to provide a valuable reinforcement of the learning.

For more details see '*The Trainer's Blue Pocketfile of ready-to-use exercises*' by John Townsend, published by Management Pocketbooks Ltd.

TECHNIQUES FOR EVALUATION

2. End of learning

Aim: to assess the trainee's opinion of the training received.

This is often carried out by the training department in the form of a questionnaire (see example on page 103).

However, managers have a key role to play at this stage by talking to their people in order to:

- Start to evaluate the worth of the training and, importantly ...
- Create a receptive environment, to encourage individuals to use their newly acquired knowledge and skills in the workplace

TECHNIQUES FOR EVALUATION

3. What has been learnt

Aim: to measure the concepts, skills and techniques that the individual has acquired.

Here you need to talk to the person who has run the training to see if they can help in devising both pre and post methods to assess this area. What better way to judge how effective their teaching has been?

However, as a manager you can help by setting up job simulations, role plays/rehearsals in order to practise skills.

For example, if the learning has focused on dealing with difficult customers, why not set up some simple scenarios to develop further the skills gained.

TECHNIQUES FOR EVALUATION

4. Measuring improvements

Aim: to discover how the individual has improved in the job as a result of the training received.

One way to do this is a three month follow-up, involving the trainer, the manager and the trainee.

Useful techniques involve making comparisons before and after the learning, as well as observing changes in behaviour.

MEASURING THE IMPACT

TECHNIQUES FOR EVALUATION

5. Impact on the organisation

Aim: to identify the benefits gained in terms of money, time and resources invested.

Often carried out by somebody from the training department, it seeks to demonstrate the value of the training to the organisation. Areas to look at include:

- Improvement in work output
- Cost savings
- Error rates
- Reduction in both the number and nature of complaints
- Improvements in quality
- Staff attitude changes

COURSE EVALUATION FORM

EXAMPLE

Course title _____ Date(s) _____

Name _____ Place of work _____ Phone No _____

We would appreciate feedback on the recent course that you attended. This will enable us to assess its usefulness and value to the organisation. Please be honest with your comments.

1. In what way was the course relevant to you? _____

2. What areas were not relevant to you? _____

3. Which subjects/sessions did you personally find **most** useful? _____

_____

Why? _____

4. Which subjects/sessions did you find **least** useful? _____

_____

Why? _____

COURSE EVALUATION FORM

EXAMPLE

5. How do you plan to put any useful learning gained into practice?

6. To apply the learning, list what help you require from:
Your boss
Your colleagues or staff
Training staff
Others (please specify)

7. What other comments do you wish to make about the training?

8. Overall, do you feel that the course was worthwhile, in terms of your time away from work?   Yes   No   Unsure

Thank you for your comments, please return this form to (name).

WHAT STOPS PEOPLE LEARNING?

Finally, if you feel that you have done everything right and people still do not seem to be learning – then there could be learning blockages, or hurdles, outside your control.
For example:

- A whole range of bad experiences at school, eg: fear of exams, boring subjects
- Age – some people feel that they are too old to learn (definitely not true)
- The jargon used
- Style of learning is unsuitable for them
- Fear of making a mistake or, worse, looking stupid
- 'Teachers' whose presentation style fails to inspire
- Sheer volume of topics to learn
- Timing – when the learning took place
- Environment not conducive
- Self imposed, ie: low self esteem and skills
- Lack of motivation: see no relevance, payoff or value in the learning

Remember, you can only do your best. You cannot force people to learn.

FURTHER READING

Trevor Bentley, *The business of training*, McGraw-Hill

Peter Bramley, *Evaluating training effectiveness*, McGraw-Hill

Roger Bennett, *Improving trainer effectiveness*, Gower

Roger Buckley and Jim Caple, *Theory and practice of training*, Kogan Page

Terence Jackson, *Evaluation: Relating training to business performance,* Kogan Page

Alan Mumford, *Management Development - strategies for action*, CIPD

Peter Honey and Alan Mumford, *The manual of learning styles*, obtainable from Ardingly House, 10 Linden Avenue, Maidenhead, Berks

A whole range of books are available under the *Management Pocketbook Series* that are suitable for the both the ad hoc and professional trainer, such as: *Coaching; Competencies; Training Evaluation and Training Needs Analysis*. See title listing at the back of the book, or visit the website (www.pocketbook.co.uk) for details.

About the Author

Ian Fleming, MA, DMS, DipEd

Ian is a freelance management trainer. His approach is to work mainly in-company, helping managers and their teams tackle real situations and opportunities. He has a preference for coaching rather than lecturing.

This pocketbook (one of six he has written) is based on his experience of helping develop people in organisations by ways other than sending them on courses.

Contact

Should you want to talk to Ian about his ideas and approach, he can be contacted at: 'Summer Bank' 38 Abbey Road, Llandudno, North Wales LL30 2EE.
Tel. 01492 877539
e-mail: ian@creativelearning.uk.com

ORDER FORM

	No. copies

Your details

Name _____

Position _____

Company _____

Address _____

_____

_____

Telephone _____

Fax _____

E-mail _____

VAT No. (EC companies) _____

Your Order Ref _____

Please send me:

The Developing People Pocketbook ☐

The _____ Pocketbook ☐

The _____ Pocketbook ☐

The _____ Pocketbook ☐

Order by Post

MANAGEMENT POCKETBOOKS LTD

LAUREL HOUSE, STATION APPROACH,
ALRESFORD, HAMPSHIRE SO24 9JH UK

Order by Phone, Fax or Internet

Telephone: +44 (0)1962 735573
Facsimile: +44 (0)1962 733637
E-mail: sales@pocketbook.co.uk
Web: www.pocketbook.co.uk

Customers in USA should contact:
Management Pocketbooks
2427 Bond Street, University Park, IL 60466
Telephone: 866 620 6944 Facsimile: 708 534 7803
E-mail: mp.orders@ware-pak.com
Web: www.managementpocketbooks.com